THIS too...

A COMPANION PLANNER

By Natalie Friscia Pancetti

Note from the Author

Ever just want to freeze time? Or maybe fast forward through the rough patches that seem to hold us down and dim our light?

The popular phrase "this too shall pass" can have so many layers with several meanings. My father taught me that this phrase, while often used for the storms in our lives, is equally important to remember during the sweet spots because they pass as well.

Time is a non-renewable resource. It cannot be bought, sold, stored, or regained. But, it can be cherished and respected enough to enjoy every moment. As I watch my boys grow up into young men, I am often reminded that time should never be taken for granted. It passes far too quickly. It needs to be collected one memory at a time. It is important to be present and savor those small moments.

I created this planner as a companion to my book *This Too...* so we can look at each day through this lens. Use the daily boxes to plan and be kind with your time.

Embrace the beautiful unpredictability of life. It's unexpected challenges, opportunities, successes, along with the twist and turns. Let's plan when we can, but always be ready to embrace "Plan B" & beyond, with flexibility, resilience, and an open mindset as we navigate all that life has to offer.

Because I'm a big fan of reflecting, each week there's space to reflect on the sweet spots and acknowledge the storms. Every four weeks there is a short quote to serve as a reminder and space for reflecting with prompts on your goals, intentions, celebrations, gratitude, connections, and, one of my favorites, signs.

It is my intention that by using this planner, you are reminded of how precious your time is, and you are inspired to make the best of this gift of life!

Happy Planning,
Natalie

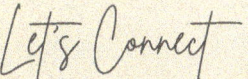

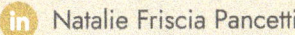 Natalie Friscia Pancetti

 @NatalieFrisciaPancetti

TAKE A

Breath

GOALS
What I'm aspiring to...

INTENTIONS
Desires I've shared with the Universe...

CELEBRATIONS
Successes to Savor...

GRATITUDE
Acknowledging my blessings...

CONNECTIONS
People I need to reach out to...

SIGNS
Messages I've received from loved ones...

Monday

Tuesday

Wednesday

Thursday

WEEK OF .... / .... / ....

Friday .... / ....

Saturday .... / ....

Sunday .... / ....

SWEET SPOTS
Things I'm grateful for

STORMS
Challenges I'm facing

Monday

Tuesday

Wednesday

Thursday

WEEK OF .... / .... / ....

Friday .... / ....

Saturday .... / ....

Sunday .... / ....

SWEET SPOTS
Things I'm grateful for

STORMS
Challenges I'm facing

Monday

Tuesday

Wednesday

Thursday

WEEK OF ..../........../..........

Friday ..../..........

Saturday ..../..........

Sunday ..../..........

SWEET SPOTS
Things I'm grateful for

STORMS
Challenges I'm facing

Monday

Tuesday

Wednesday

Thursday

WEEK OF .... / ..... / ....

/

Friday

/

Saturday

/

Sunday

SWEET SPOTS
Things I'm grateful for

STORMS
Challenges I'm facing

GOALS

What I'm aspiring to...

....
....
....
....
....
....
....
....

INTENTIONS

Desires I've shared with the Universe...

....
....
....
....
....
....
....
....

CELEBRATIONS

Successes to Savor...

....
....
....
....
....
....
....
....

GRATITUDE

Acknowledging my blessings...

....
....
....
....
....
....
....
....

CONNECTIONS

People I need to reach out to...

....
....
....
....
....
....
....
....

SIGNS

Messages I've received from loved ones...

....
....
....
....
....
....
....
....

Monday

/

Tuesday

/

Wednesday

/

Thursday

/

WEEK OF ___ / ___ / ___

Friday ___ / ___

Saturday ___ / ___

Sunday ___ / ___

SWEET SPOTS
Things I'm grateful for

STORMS
Challenges I'm facing

Monday

/

Tuesday

/

Wednesday

/

Thursday

/

WEEK OF _____ / _____ / _____

Friday _____ / _____

Saturday _____ / _____

Sunday _____ / _____

SWEET SPOTS
Things I'm grateful for

STORMS
Challenges I'm facing

Monday ..../........

Tuesday ..../........

Wednesday ..../........

Thursday ..../........

WEEK OF .... / .... / ....

Friday .... / ....

Saturday .... / ....

Sunday .... / ....

SWEET SPOTS
Things I'm grateful for

STORMS
Challenges I'm facing

Monday

......./.......

Tuesday

......./.......

Wednesday

......./.......

Thursday

......./.......

WEEK OF .... / .... / ....

Friday .... / ....

Saturday .... / ....

Sunday .... / ....

SWEET SPOTS
Things I'm grateful for

STORMS
Challenges I'm facing

LIGHTEN

Your

Load

GOALS

What I'm aspiring to...

_____
_____
_____
_____
_____
_____
_____
_____
_____

INTENTIONS

Desires I've shared with the Universe...

_____
_____
_____
_____
_____
_____
_____
_____
_____

CELEBRATIONS

Successes to Savor...

_____
_____
_____
_____
_____
_____
_____
_____
_____

GRATITUDE

Acknowledging my blessings...

_____
_____
_____
_____
_____
_____
_____
_____
_____

CONNECTIONS

People I need to reach out to...

_____
_____
_____
_____
_____
_____
_____
_____
_____

SIGNS

Messages I've received from loved ones...

_____
_____
_____
_____
_____
_____
_____
_____
_____

Monday

......../........

Tuesday

......../........

Wednesday

......../........

Thursday

......../........

WEEK OF .... / ..... / ....

Friday .... / ....

Saturday .... / ....

Sunday .... / ....

SWEET SPOTS
Things I'm grateful for

STORMS
Challenges I'm facing

Monday

_____ / _____

Tuesday

_____ / _____

Wednesday

_____ / _____

Thursday

_____ / _____

WEEK OF .... / .... / ....

Friday .... / ....

Saturday .... / ....

Sunday .... / ....

SWEET SPOTS
Things I'm grateful for

STORMS
Challenges I'm facing

Monday

Tuesday

Wednesday

Thursday

WEEK OF .... / .... / ....

.... / ....
Friday

.... / ....
Saturday

.... / ....
Sunday

SWEET SPOTS
Things I'm grateful for

STORMS
Challenges I'm facing

Monday

Tuesday

Wednesday

Thursday

WEEK OF .... / .... / ....

...... / ......
Friday

...... / ......
Saturday

...... / ......
Sunday

SWEET SPOTS
Things I'm grateful for

STORMS
Challenges I'm facing

POSITIVITY IS

Priceless

GOALS
What I'm aspiring to...

INTENTIONS
Desires I've shared with the Universe...

CELEBRATIONS
Successes to Savor...

GRATITUDE
Acknowledging my blessings...

CONNECTIONS
People I need to reach out to...

SIGNS
Messages I've received from loved ones...

Monday ..../........

Tuesday ..../........

Wednesday ..../........

Thursday ..../........

WEEK OF .... / .... / ....

Friday .... / ....

Saturday .... / ....

Sunday .... / ....

SWEET SPOTS
Things I'm grateful for

STORMS
Challenges I'm facing

Monday

......../........

Tuesday

......../........

Wednesday

......../........

Thursday

......../........

WEEK OF .... / .... / ....

Friday .... / ....

Saturday .... / ....

Sunday .... / ....

SWEET SPOTS
Things I'm grateful for

STORMS
Challenges I'm facing

Monday

 /

Tuesday

 /

Wednesday

 /

Thursday

 /

WEEK OF ____ / ____ / ____

Friday ____ / ____

Saturday ____ / ____

Sunday ____ / ____

SWEET SPOTS
Things I'm grateful for

STORMS
Challenges I'm facing

Monday

........../..........

Tuesday

........../..........

Wednesday

........../..........

Thursday

........../..........

WEEK OF .... / .... / ....

.... / ....
Friday

.... / ....
Saturday

.... / ....
Sunday

SWEET SPOTS
Things I'm grateful for

STORMS
Challenges I'm facing

YOUR
BRIGHTNESS
IS

Your Bravery

GOALS
What I'm aspiring to...

INTENTIONS
Desires I've shared with the Universe...

CELEBRATIONS
Successes to Savor...

GRATITUDE
Acknowledging my blessings...

CONNECTIONS
People I need to reach out to...

SIGNS
Messages I've received from loved ones...

Monday

.... / ....

Tuesday

.... / ....

Wednesday

.... / ....

Thursday

.... / ....

WEEK OF .... / .... / ....

Friday
.... / ....

Saturday
.... / ....

Sunday
.... / ....

SWEET SPOTS
Things I'm grateful for

STORMS
Challenges I'm facing

Monday

/

Tuesday

/

Wednesday

/

Thursday

/

WEEK OF .... / .... / ....

Friday   .... / ....

Saturday   .... / ....

Sunday   .... / ....

SWEET SPOTS
Things I'm grateful for

STORMS
Challenges I'm facing

Monday

.... / ....

Tuesday

.... / ....

Wednesday

.... / ....

Thursday

.... / ....

WEEK OF .... / .... / ....

.... / ....

Friday

.... / ....

Saturday

.... / ....

Sunday

SWEET SPOTS
Things I'm grateful for

STORMS
Challenges I'm facing

Monday

Tuesday

Wednesday

Thursday

WEEK OF .... / .... / ....

Friday .... / ....

Saturday .... / ....

Sunday .... / ....

SWEET SPOTS
Things I'm grateful for

STORMS
Challenges I'm facing

KEEP THE FAITH
AND THE FAITH

*Will
Keep You*

GOALS
What I'm aspiring to...

INTENTIONS
Desires I've shared with the Universe...

CELEBRATIONS
Successes to Savor...

GRATITUDE
Acknowledging my blessings...

CONNECTIONS
People I need to reach out to...

SIGNS
Messages I've received from loved ones...

.... / ....

Monday

.... / ....

Tuesday

.... / ....

Wednesday

.... / ....

Thursday

WEEK OF ____ / ____ / ____

Friday ____ / ____

Saturday ____ / ____

Sunday ____ / ____

SWEET SPOTS
Things I'm grateful for

STORMS
Challenges I'm facing

Monday ..... / .....

Tuesday ..... / .....

Wednesday ..... / .....

Thursday ..... / .....

WEEK OF .... / .... / ....

Friday .... / ....

Saturday .... / ....

Sunday .... / ....

SWEET SPOTS
Things I'm grateful for

STORMS
Challenges I'm facing

Monday

Tuesday

Wednesday

Thursday

WEEK OF ..../......../........

............/........

Friday

............/........

Saturday

............/........

Sunday

SWEET SPOTS
Things I'm grateful for

STORMS
Challenges I'm facing

Monday

_____ / _____

Tuesday

_____ / _____

Wednesday

_____ / _____

Thursday

_____ / _____

WEEK OF ..... / ..... / .....

Friday ..... / .....

Saturday ..... / .....

Sunday ..... / .....

SWEET SPOTS
Things I'm grateful for

STORMS
Challenges I'm facing

PERSPECTIVE

Helps Us Pivot

GOALS

What I'm aspiring to...

INTENTIONS

Desires I've shared with the Universe...

CELEBRATIONS

Successes to Savor...

GRATITUDE

Acknowledging my blessings...

CONNECTIONS

People I need to reach out to...

SIGNS

Messages I've received from loved ones...

Monday

Tuesday

Wednesday

Thursday

WEEK OF .... / ...... / ....

Friday
.... / ......

Saturday
.... / ......

Sunday
.... / ......

SWEET SPOTS
Things I'm grateful for

STORMS
Challenges I'm facing

Monday

___ / ___

Tuesday

___ / ___

Wednesday

___ / ___

Thursday

WEEK OF .... / .... / ....

Friday .... / ....

Saturday .... / ....

Sunday .... / ....

SWEET SPOTS
Things I'm grateful for

STORMS
Challenges I'm facing

Monday

___ / ___

Tuesday

___ / ___

Wednesday

___ / ___

Thursday

___ / ___

WEEK OF .... / .... / ....

Friday   .... / ....

Saturday   .... / ....

Sunday   .... / ....

SWEET SPOTS
Things I'm grateful for

STORMS
Challenges I'm facing

Monday

................/................

Tuesday

................/................

Wednesday

................/................

Thursday

................/................

WEEK OF ____/____/____

Friday ____/____

Saturday ____/____

Sunday ____/____

SWEET SPOTS
Things I'm grateful for

STORMS
Challenges I'm facing

KNOW

Your

Worth

GOALS
What I'm aspiring to...

_____
_____
_____
_____
_____
_____
_____
_____

INTENTIONS
Desires I've shared with the Universe...

_____
_____
_____
_____
_____
_____
_____
_____

CELEBRATIONS
Successes to Savor...

_____
_____
_____
_____
_____
_____
_____
_____

GRATITUDE
Acknowledging my blessings...

_____
_____
_____
_____
_____
_____
_____
_____

CONNECTIONS
People I need to reach out to...

_____
_____
_____
_____
_____
_____
_____
_____

SIGNS
Messages I've received from loved ones...

_____
_____
_____
_____
_____
_____
_____
_____

Monday

.........../...........

Tuesday

.........../...........

Wednesday

.........../...........

Thursday

.........../...........

WEEK OF .... / .... / ....

Friday .... / ....

Saturday .... / ....

Sunday .... / ....

SWEET SPOTS
Things I'm grateful for

STORMS
Challenges I'm facing

Monday

Tuesday

Wednesday

Thursday

WEEK OF .... / .... / ....

Friday .... / ....

Saturday .... / ....

Sunday .... / ....

SWEET SPOTS
Things I'm grateful for

STORMS
Challenges I'm facing

Monday

/

Tuesday

/

Wednesday

/

Thursday

/

WEEK OF .... / .... / ....

Friday .... / ....

Saturday .... / ....

Sunday .... / ....

SWEET SPOTS
Things I'm grateful for

STORMS
Challenges I'm facing

Monday

_____ / _____

Tuesday

_____ / _____

Wednesday

_____ / _____

Thursday

_____ / _____

WEEK OF .... / ...... / ....

Friday .... / ....

Saturday .... / ....

Sunday .... / ....

SWEET SPOTS
Things I'm grateful for

STORMS
Challenges I'm facing

GOALS
What I'm aspiring to...

INTENTIONS
Desires I've shared with the Universe...

CELEBRATIONS
Successes to Savor...

GRATITUDE
Acknowledging my blessings...

CONNECTIONS
People I need to reach out to...

SIGNS
Messages I've received from loved ones...

Monday ..... / .....

Tuesday ..... / .....

Wednesday ..... / .....

Thursday ..... / .....

WEEK OF ..../......../........

Friday ..../........

Saturday ..../........

Sunday ..../........

SWEET SPOTS
Things I'm grateful for

STORMS
Challenges I'm facing

Monday   /

Tuesday   /

Wednesday   /

Thursday   /

WEEK OF ____ / ____ / ____

Friday
____ / ____

Saturday
____ / ____

Sunday
____ / ____

SWEET SPOTS
Things I'm grateful for

STORMS
Challenges I'm facing

Monday ..... / .....

Tuesday ..... / .....

Wednesday ..... / .....

Thursday ..... / .....

WEEK OF   /   /

Friday   /

Saturday   /

Sunday   /

SWEET SPOTS
Things I'm grateful for

STORMS
Challenges I'm facing

Monday

......../........

Tuesday

......../........

Wednesday

......../........

Thursday

......../........

WEEK OF .... / .... / ....

Friday .... / ....

Saturday .... / ....

Sunday .... / ....

SWEET SPOTS
Things I'm grateful for

STORMS
Challenges I'm facing

CELEBRATE

Your Successes

GOALS

What I'm aspiring to...

INTENTIONS

Desires I've shared with the Universe...

CELEBRATIONS

Successes to Savor...

GRATITUDE

Acknowledging my blessings...

CONNECTIONS

People I need to reach out to...

SIGNS

Messages I've received from loved ones...

Monday ..../........

Tuesday ..../........

Wednesday ..../........

Thursday ..../........

WEEK OF ..../......../........

Friday ..../........

Saturday ..../........

Sunday ..../........

SWEET SPOTS
Things I'm grateful for

STORMS
Challenges I'm facing

Monday

Tuesday

Wednesday

Thursday

WEEK OF .... / .... / ....

Friday .... / ....

Saturday .... / ....

Sunday .... / ....

SWEET SPOTS
Things I'm grateful for

STORMS
Challenges I'm facing

Monday

Tuesday

Wednesday

Thursday

WEEK OF .... / .... / ....

Friday
.... / ....

Saturday
.... / ....

Sunday
.... / ....

SWEET SPOTS
Things I'm grateful for

STORMS
Challenges I'm facing

Monday

    /

Tuesday

    /

Wednesday

    /

Thursday

    /

WEEK OF .... / .... / ....

Friday .... / ....

Saturday .... / ....

Sunday .... / ....

SWEET SPOTS
Things I'm grateful for

STORMS
Challenges I'm facing

GOALS
What I'm aspiring to...

INTENTIONS
Desires I've shared with the Universe...

CELEBRATIONS
Successes to Savor...

GRATITUDE
Acknowledging my blessings...

CONNECTIONS
People I need to reach out to...

SIGNS
Messages I've received from loved ones...

Monday   /

Tuesday   /

Wednesday   /

Thursday   /

WEEK OF .... / .... / ....

Friday .... / ....

Saturday .... / ....

Sunday .... / ....

SWEET SPOTS
Things I'm grateful for

STORMS
Challenges I'm facing

Monday

_____ / _____

Tuesday

_____ / _____

Wednesday

_____ / _____

Thursday

_____ / _____

WEEK OF .... / .... / ....

Friday .... / ....

Saturday .... / ....

Sunday .... / ....

SWEET SPOTS
Things I'm grateful for

STORMS
Challenges I'm facing

Monday ..../........

Tuesday ..../........

Wednesday ..../........

Thursday ..../........

WEEK OF .... / .... / ....

Friday .... / ....

Saturday .... / ....

Sunday .... / ....

SWEET SPOTS
Things I'm grateful for

STORMS
Challenges I'm facing

Monday ____ / ____

Tuesday ____ / ____

Wednesday ____ / ____

Thursday ____ / ____

WEEK OF .... / .... / ....

Friday .... / ....

Saturday .... / ....

Sunday .... / ....

SWEET SPOTS
Things I'm grateful for

STORMS
Challenges I'm facing

REALIZE

What's Possible

GOALS

What I'm aspiring to...

INTENTIONS

Desires I've shared with the Universe...

CELEBRATIONS

Successes to Savor...

GRATITUDE

Acknowledging my blessings...

CONNECTIONS

People I need to reach out to...

SIGNS

Messages I've received from loved ones...

Monday

___ / ___

Tuesday

___ / ___

Wednesday

___ / ___

Thursday

___ / ___

WEEK OF .... / .... / ....

.... / ....

Friday

.... / ....

Saturday

.... / ....

Sunday

SWEET SPOTS
Things I'm grateful for

STORMS
Challenges I'm facing

Monday

Tuesday

Wednesday

Thursday

WEEK OF .... / ...... / ....

.... / ....
Friday

.... / ....
Saturday

.... / ....
Sunday

SWEET SPOTS	STORMS
Things I'm grateful for	*Challenges I'm facing*

Monday

/

Tuesday

/

Wednesday

/

Thursday

/

WEEK OF .... / .... / ....

Friday .... / ....

Saturday .... / ....

Sunday .... / ....

SWEET SPOTS
Things I'm grateful for

STORMS
Challenges I'm facing

Monday

Tuesday

Wednesday

Thursday

WEEK OF ____ / ____ / ____

Friday
____ / ____

Saturday
____ / ____

Sunday
____ / ____

SWEET SPOTS
Things I'm grateful for

STORMS
Challenges I'm facing

GOALS

What I'm aspiring to...

....
....
....
....
....
....
....
....
....
....

INTENTIONS

Desires I've shared with the Universe...

....
....
....
....
....
....
....
....
....
....

CELEBRATIONS

Successes to Savor...

....
....
....
....
....
....
....
....
....
....

GRATITUDE

Acknowledging my blessings...

....
....
....
....
....
....
....
....
....
....

CONNECTIONS

People I need to reach out to...

....
....
....
....
....
....
....
....
....
....

SIGNS

Messages I've received from loved ones...

....
....
....
....
....
....
....
....
....
....

Monday

_____ / _____

Tuesday

_____ / _____

Wednesday

_____ / _____

Thursday

WEEK OF .... / .... / ....

.... / ....
Friday

.... / ....
Saturday

.... / ....
Sunday

SWEET SPOTS
Things I'm grateful for

STORMS
Challenges I'm facing

Monday

_____ / _____

Tuesday

_____ / _____

Wednesday

_____ / _____

Thursday

WEEK OF   /   /

Friday   /

Saturday   /

Sunday   /

SWEET SPOTS
Things I'm grateful for

STORMS
Challenges I'm facing

Monday

/

Tuesday

/

Wednesday

/

Thursday

/

WEEK OF ___ / ___ / ___

Friday ___ / ___

Saturday ___ / ___

Sunday ___ / ___

SWEET SPOTS
Things I'm grateful for

STORMS
Challenges I'm facing

Monday

.... / ....

Tuesday

.... / ....

Wednesday

.... / ....

Thursday

.... / ....

WEEK OF .... / .... / ....

Friday .... / ....

Saturday .... / ....

Sunday .... / ....

SWEET SPOTS
Things I'm grateful for

STORMS
Challenges I'm facing

COPYRIGHT PAGE

This Too... A Companion Planner by Natalie Friscia Pancetti

Published by IG Introspections, an imprint of Inspired Girl Publishing Group,
a division of Inspired Girl Enterprises.
Asbury Park, NJ
www.inspiredgirlbooks.com

Inspired Girl Books is honored to bring forth books with heart and stories that matter. We are proud to offer this book to our readers; the theme, the life- isms, the thoughts, and the words are the author's alone. The author and publisher do not assume and hereby disclaim any liability in connection with the use of the information contained in this book.

No endorsement of the information contained in this book is given by the owners of products and trademarks used in this book, and no endorsement is implied by the inclusion of products, books, or trademarks in this book.

© 2024 Natalie Friscia Pancetti
All rights reserved. No portion of this book may be reproduced in any form without permission from the publisher, except as permitted by U.S. copyright law.

For permissions contact:
help@inspiredgirlbooks.com

ISBN: 978-1-965240-00-7
Editorial and Creative Direction by Jenn Tuma-Young
Written by Natalie Friscia Pancetti

Printed in the USA.

www.ingramcontent.com/pod-product-compliance
Lightning Source LLC
Chambersburg PA
CBHW040307170426
43194CB00022B/2930